BOB DYLAN
MADE EASY FOR GUITAR

COVER PHOTOGRAPHY BY KEN REGAN/CAMERA 5

THIS BOOK COPYRIGHT © 1994 BY SPECIAL RIDER MUSIC

ORDER NO. AM 86112

ISBN 978-0-8256-1416-3

EXCLUSIVELY DISTRIBUTED BY

HAL•LEONARD®

Blowin' In The Wind

Words and Music by Bob Dylan

Moderately

1. How man-y roads must a man walk down be-fore you call him a man? Yes, 'n' how man-y seas must a white dove sail be-fore she sleeps in the sand? Yes, 'n' how man-y times must the can-non balls fly be-fore they're for-ev-er banned? The an-swer, my friend, is

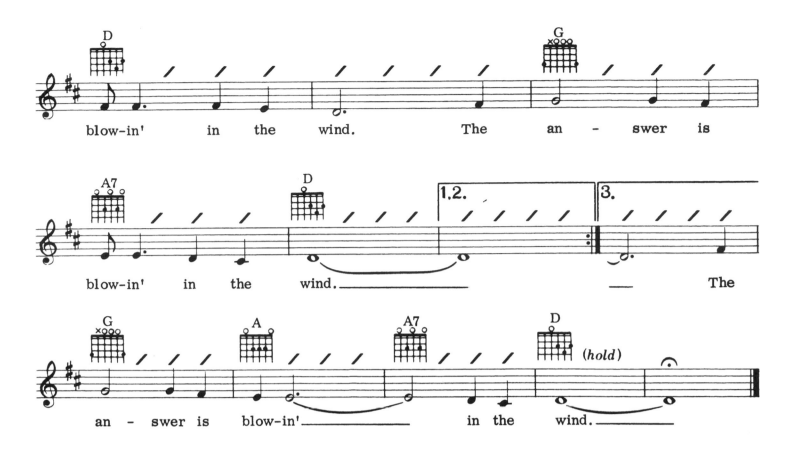

blow-in'   in   the   wind.   The   an - swer   is

blow-in'   in   the   wind.＿＿＿＿＿   ＿   The

an - swer   is   blow-in'＿＿＿＿   in   the   wind.＿＿＿＿

Additional lyrics

2. How many times must a man look up
   Before he can see the sky?
   Yes, 'n' how many ears must one man have
   Before he can hear people cry?
   Yes, 'n' how many deaths will it take till he knows
   That too many people have died?

3. How many years can a mountain exist
   Before it's washed to the sea?
   Yes, 'n' how many years can some people exist
   Before they're allowed to be free?
   Yes, 'n' how many times can a man turn his head
   Pretending he just doesn't see?

Mr. Tambourine Man
Words and Music by Bob Dylan

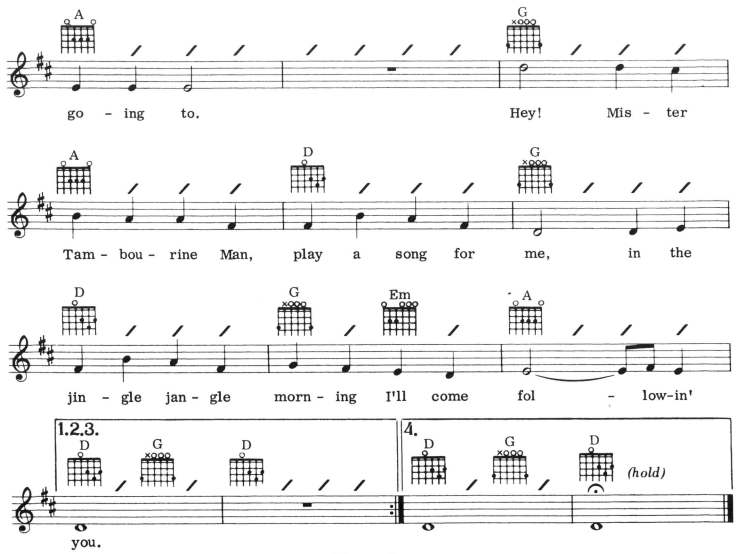

go - ing to. Hey! Mis - ter

Tam - bou - rine Man, play a song for me, in the

jin - gle jan - gle morn - ing I'll come fol - low-in'

1.2.3.

4.

(hold)

you.

Additional lyrics

2. Take me on a trip upon your magic swirlin' ship.
   My senses have been stripped, my hands can't feel to grip,
   My toes too numb to step, wait only for my boot heels
   To be wanderin'.
   I'm ready to go anywhere, I'm ready for to fade
   Into my own parade, cast your dancing spell my way;
   I promise to go under it.

3. Though you might hear laughin', spinnin', swingin' madly across the sun,
   It's not aimed at anyone, it's just escapin' on the run.
   And but for the sky there are no fences facin'.
   And if you hear vague traces of skippin' reels of rhyme
   To your tambourine in time, it's just a ragged clown behind.
   I wouldn't pay it any mind, it's just a shadow you're
   Seein' that he's chasing.

4. Then take me disappearin' through the smoke rings of my mind,
   Down the foggy ruins of time, far past the frozen leaves,
   The haunted, frightened trees, out to the windy beach
   Far from the twisted reach of crazy sorrow.
   Yes, to dance beneath the diamond sky with one hand waving free,
   Silhouetted by the sea, circled by the circus sands,
   With all memory and fate, driven deep beneath the waves.
   Let me forget about today until tomorrow.

Man Gave Names To All The Animals
Words and Music by Bob Dylan

Words and Music by
BOB DYLAN

Moderately fast

Man gave names to all the an-i-mals, in the be-gin-ning, in the be-gin-ning.

Man gave names to all the an-i-mals, in the be-gin-ning,

long time a-go.

1. He saw an an-i-mal that liked to growl.

Big fur-ry paws, and he liked to

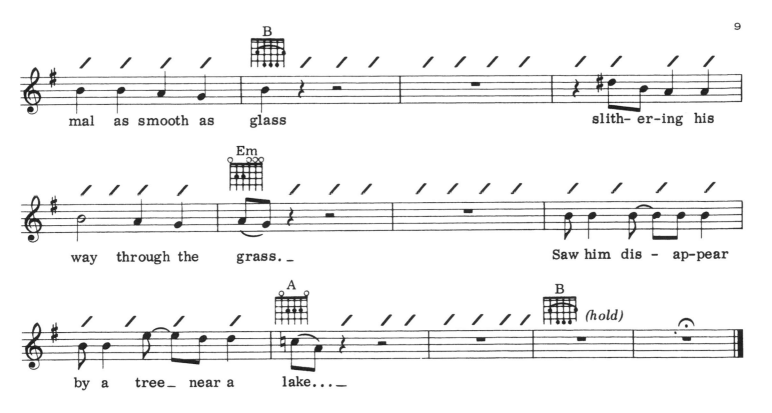

mal as smooth as glass slith- er-ing his

way through the grass. _ Saw him dis - ap-pear

by a tree _ near a lake... _

Additional lyrics

3. He saw an animal up on a hill
   Chewing up so much grass until she was filled.
   He saw milk comin' out, but he didn't know how.
   "Ah, think I'll call it a cow."

3. He saw an animal that liked to snort.
   Horns on his head and they weren't too short.
   It looked like there wasn't nothin' that he couldn't pull.
   "Ah, think I'll call it a bull."

4. He saw an animal leavin' a muddy trail.
   Real dirty face and a curly tail.
   He wasn't too small and he wasn't too big.
   "Ah, think I'll call it a pig."

5. Next animal that he did meet
   Had wool on his back and hooves on his feet.
   Eating grass on a mountainside so steep.
   "Ah, think I'll call it a sheep."

Just Like A Woman

Words and Music by Bob Dylan

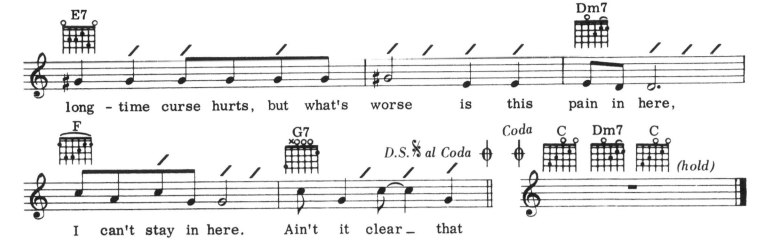

dy-ing there of thirst, so I came in here. And your long-time curse hurts, but what's worse is this pain in here, I can't stay in here. Ain't it clear — that

Additional lyrics

2.   Queen Mary, she's my friend.
Yes, I believe I'll go see her again,
Nobody has to guess that Baby can't be blessed
Till she sees finally that she's like all the rest
With her fog, her amphetamines and her pearls.

She takes just like a woman, yes, she does.
She makes love just like a woman, yes, she does.
And she aches just lika a woman,
But she breaks just like a little girl.

3.   I just can't fit.
Yes, I believe it's time for us to quit.
When we meet again introduced as friends,
Please don't let on that you knew me when
I was hungry and it was your world.

Ah, you fake just like a woman, yes, you do.
You make love just like a woman, yes, you do.
Then you ache just like a woman,
But you break just like a little girl.

Don't Think Twice, It's All Right

Words and Music by Bob Dylan

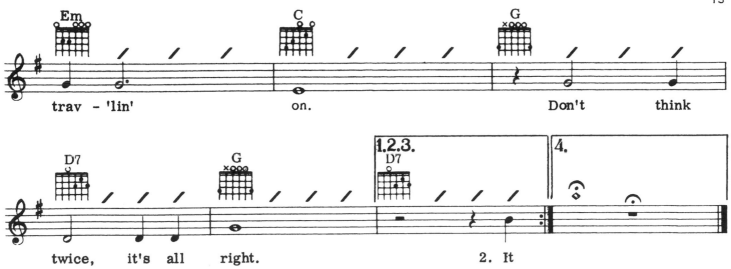

trav - 'lin'   on.   Don't   think

twice,   it's   all   right.   2. It

Additional lyrics

2. It ain't no use in turnin' on your light, babe,
   That light I never knowed.
   An' it ain't no use in turnin' on your light, babe,
   I'm on the dark side of the road.
   Still, I wish there was somethin' you would do or say
   To try and make me change my mind and stay.
   We never did too much talkin' anyway.
   So don't think twice, it's all right.

3. It ain't no use in callin' out my name, gal,
   Like you never did before.
   It ain't no use in callin' out my name, gal,
   I can't hear you any more.
   I'm a-thinkin' and a-wond'rin' all the way down the road,
   I once loved a woman, a child I'm told.
   I give her my heart, but she wanted my soul.
   But don't think twice, it's all right.

4. I'm walkin' down that long, lonesome road, babe,
   Where I'm bound I can't tell.
   But goodbye's too good a word, gal,
   So I'll just say fare thee well.
   I ain't sayin' you treated me unkind.
   You could have done better, but I don't mind.
   You just kind-a wasted my precious time.
   But don't think twice, it's all right.

WHEN THE SHIP COMES IN

WORDS AND MUSIC BY BOB DYLAN

Moderately

1. Oh, the time will come up when the winds will stop and the breeze will cease to be breath - in'_____ Like the still -ness in the wind 'fore the hur - ri - cane be -gins, the ho - ur when the ship comes in. Oh, the seas will split and the ship will hit and the sands on the shore-line will be shak- ing._____ Then the tide will sound and the wind will pound and the

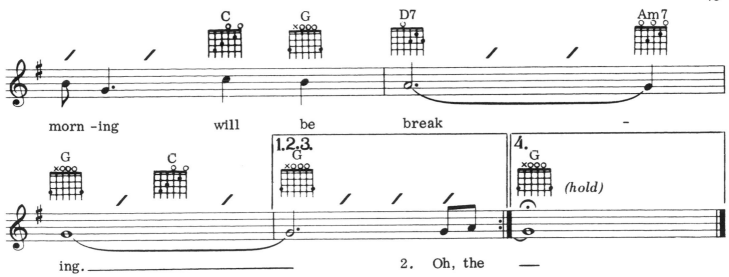

morn -ing   will   be   break   -

ing. _____   2. Oh, the ___

(hold)

Additional lyrics

2. Oh, the fishes will laugh
    As they swim out of the path
    And the seagulls they'll be smiling.
    And the rocks on the sand
    Will proudly stand
    The hour that the ship comes in.
    And the words that are used
    For to get the ship confused
    Will not be understood as they're spoken.
    For the chains of the sea
    Will have busted in the night
    And will be buried at the bottom of the ocean.

3. A song will lift
    As the mainsail shifts
    And the boat drifts on to the shore line.
    And the sun will respect
    Every face on the deck
    The hour that the ships comes in.
    Then the sands will roll
    Out a carpet of gold
    For your weary toes to be a-touchin'.
    And the ship's wise men
    Will remind you once again
    That the whole wide world is watchin'.

4. Oh, the foes will rise
    With the sleep still in their eyes
    And they'll jerk from their beds and think they're dreamin'.
    But they'll pinch themselves and squeal
    And know that it's for real,
    The hour when the ship comes in.
    Then they'll raise their hands
    Sayin', We'll meet all your demands,
    But we'll shout from the bow your days are numbered.
    And like Pharoah's tribe
    They'll be drownded in the tide
    And like Goliath they'll be conquered.

Mozambique

Words and Music by Bob Dylan/Jacques Levy

Moderate Reggae beat

I like to spend some time ___ in Mo - zam-bique.
There's lots of pret - ty girls ___ in Mo - zam-bique.

The sun - ny sky is aq - ua-blue.
and plen - ty time for good ___ ro-mance.

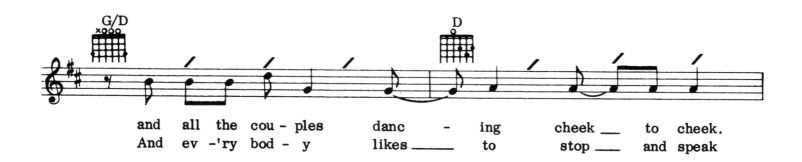

and all the cou - ples danc - ing cheek ___ to cheek.
And ev -'ry bod - y likes ___ to stop ___ and speak

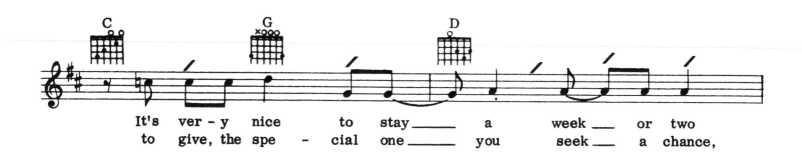

It's ver - y nice to stay ___ a week ___ or two
to give, the spe - cial one ___ you seek ___ a chance,

and may - be fall in love, ___ just me ___ and you.
or may - be say hel - lo ___ with just ___ a glance.

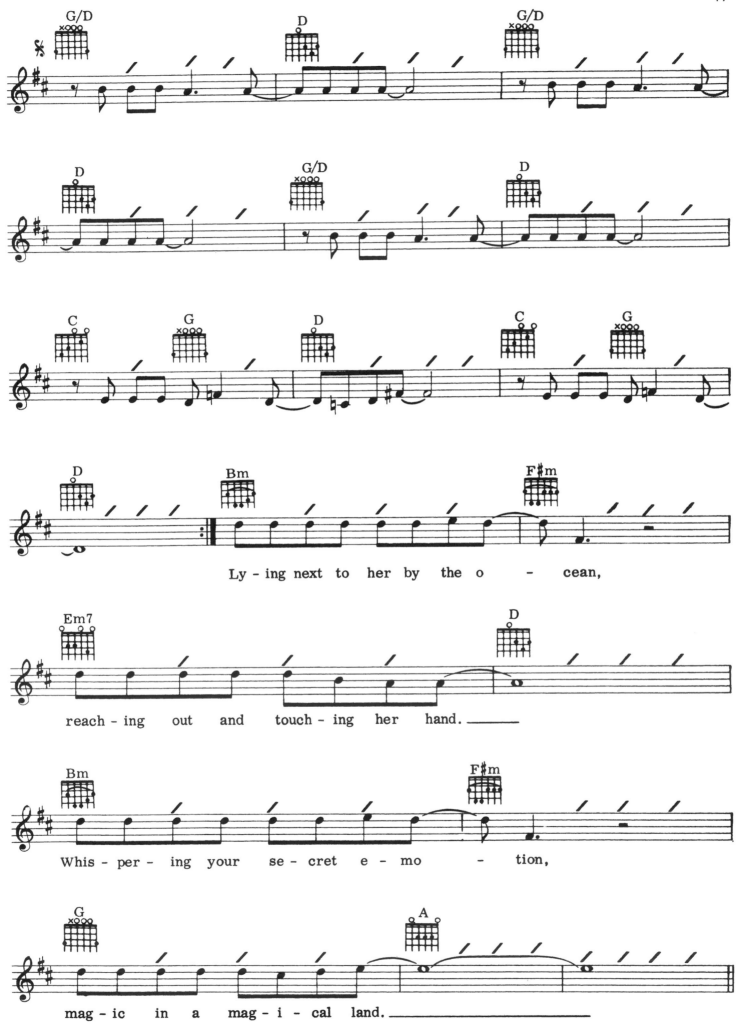

Ly - ing next to her by the o - cean,

reach - ing out and touch - ing her hand.

Whis - per - ing your se - cret e - mo - tion,

mag - ic in a mag - i - cal land.

Like A Rolling Stone

Words and Music by Bob Dylan

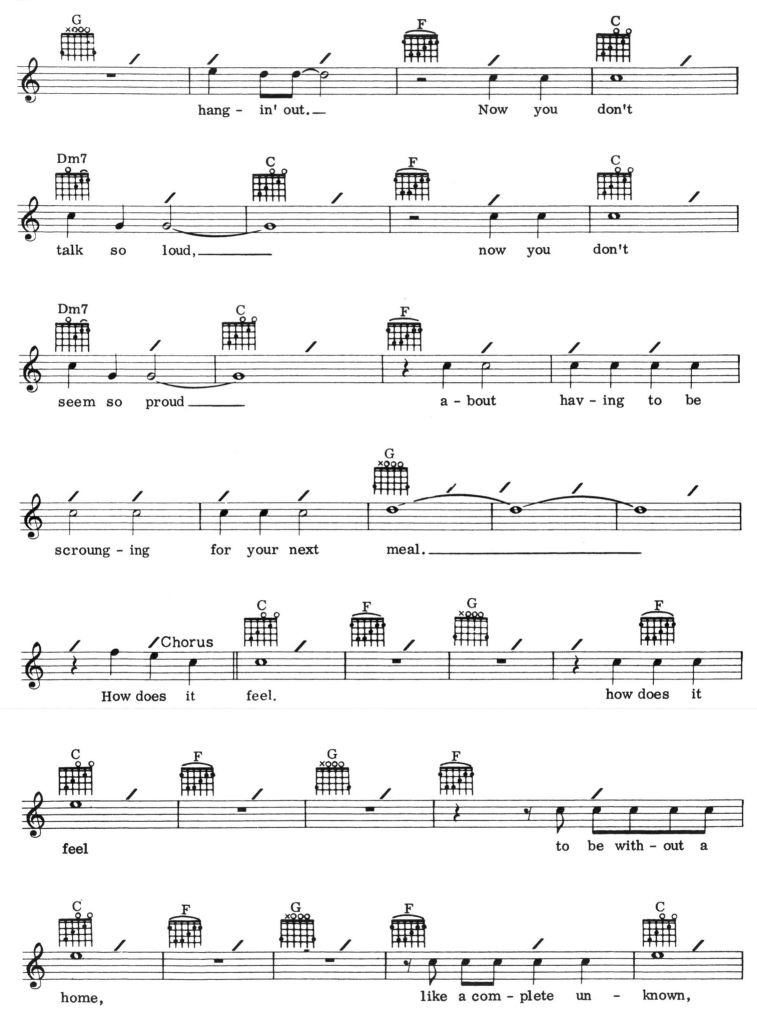

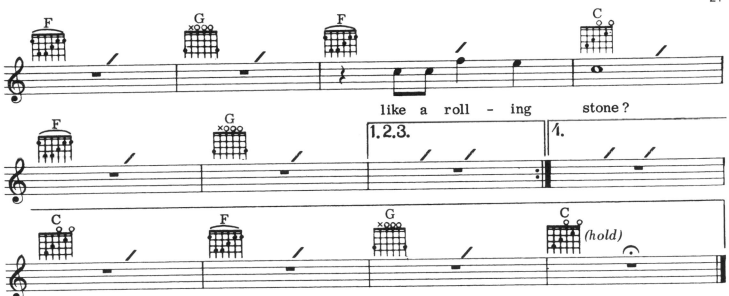

like a roll - ing stone?

Additional lyrics

2. You've gone to the finest school all right Miss Lonely,
   But you know you only used to get
   Juiced in it.
   And nobody has ever taught you how to live on the street
   And now you find out you're gonna have to get
   Used to it.
   You said you'd never compromise
   With the mystery tramp, but now you realize
   He's not selling any alibis
   As you stare into the vacuum of his eyes
   And ask him do you want to
   Make a deal?

   Chorus { Ho does it feel
   How does it feel
   To be on your own
   With no direction home
   Like a complete unknown
   Like a rolling stone? }

3. You never turned around to see the frowns on the jugglers and the clowns
   When they all come down
   And did tricks for you.
   You never understood that it ain't no good,
   You shouldn't let other people
   Get your kicks for you.
   You used to ride on the chrome horse with your diplomat
   Who carried on his shoulder a Siamese cat,
   Ain't it hard when you discovered that
   He really wasn't where it's at
   After he took from you everything
   He could steal.

   Chorus { How does it feel
   How does it feel
   To be on your own
   With no direction home
   Like a complete unknown
   Like a rolling stone? }

4. Princess on the steeple
   And all the pretty people, they're drinkin', thinkin'
   That they got it made.
   Exchanging all kinds of precious gifts and things,
   But you'd better lift your diamond ring,
   You'd better pawn it babe.
   You used to be so amused
   At Napoleon in rags and the language that he used.
   Go to him now, he calls you, you can't refuse.
   When you got nothing, you got nothing to lose.
   You're invisible now, you got no secrets
   To conceal.

   Chorus { How does it feel
   How does it feel
   To be on your own
   With no direction home
   Like a complete unknown
   Like a rolling stone? }

The Times They Are A-Changin'

Words and Music by Bob Dylan

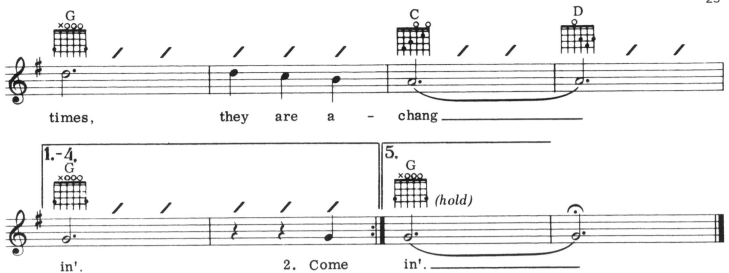

times, they are a - chang_____

1.-4. in'. 2. Come in'. _____

Additional lyrics

2. Come writers and critics
   Who prophesize with your pen.
   And keep your eyes wide,
   The chance won't come again.
   And don't speak too soon
   For the wheel's still in spin,
   And there's no tellin' who
   That it's namin'.
   For the loser now
   Will be later to win,
   For the times, they are a-changin'.

3. Come senators, congressmen,
   Please heed the call.
   Don't stand in the doorway,
   Don't block up the hall.
   For he that gets hurt
   Will be he who has stalled.
   There's a battle
   Outside and it is ragin'.
   It'll soon shake your windows
   And rattle your walls,
   For the times, they are a-changin'.

4. Come mothers and fathers
   Throughout the land.
   And don't criticize
   What you can't understand.
   Your sons and your daughters
   Are beyond your command.
   Your old road is
   Rapidly agin'.
   Please get out of the new one
   If you can't lend your hand,
   For the times, they are a-changin'.

5. The line it is drawn,
   The curse it is cast.
   The slow one now will
   Later be fast,
   As the present now
   Will later be past.
   The order is rapidly fadin'.
   And the first one now
   Will later be last,
   For the times, they are a-changin'.

All I Really Want To Do

Words and Music by Bob Dylan

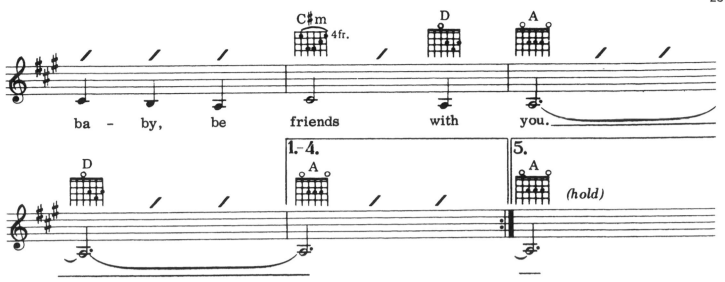

ba - by, be friends with you._____

Additional lyrics

2. No, and I ain't lookin' to fight with you
   Frighten you, or tighten you,
   Drag you down, or drain you down,
   Chain you down, or bring you down.

3. I ain't lookin' to block you up,
   Shock or knock or lock you up,
   Analyze you, categorize you,
   Finalize you or advertise you.

4. I don't want to straight-face you,
   Race, or chase you, track or trace you,
   Or disgrace you, or displace you,
   Or define you, or confine you.

5. I don't want to meet your kin,
   Make you spin, or do you in,
   Or select you, or dissect you,
   Or inspect you, or reject you.

6. I don't want to fake you out,
   Take, or shake or forsake you out,
   I ain't lookin' for you to feel like me,
   See like me, or be like me.

Saved

Words and Music by Bob Dylan

Medium Gospel beat

1. I was blind-ed by the dev-il, born al-read-y ruined;

stone - cold dead as I stepped out of the womb. By His

grace I have been touched. By His word I have been healed. By His

hand I've been de-liv-ered. By His Spir-it I've been sealed. I've been

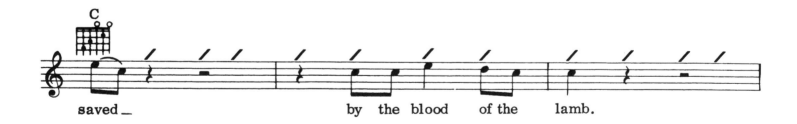

saved by the blood of the lamb.

Saved by the blood of the

lamb.   Saved. _

Saved. _   And I'm   so glad.

Yes, I'm   so glad. _   I'm   so glad. _

So glad. _   I   want to

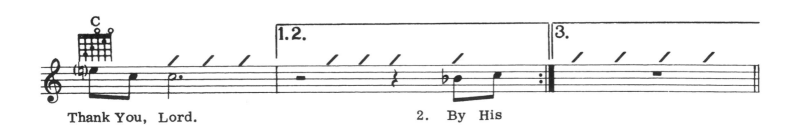

thank You, Lord   I   just want to   thank You, Lord.

Thank You, Lord.   2. By His

Repeat and fade

Thank You, Lord.   Thank You, Lord.

Thank You,   Lord.

Additional lyrics

2. By His truth I can be upright.
   By His strength I do endure.
   By His power I've been lifted.
   In His love I am secure.
   He bought me with a price:
   Freed me from the pit
   Full of emptiness and wrath
   And the fire that burns in it.

3. Nobody to rescue me,
   Nobody would dare.
   I was going down for the last time,
   But by His mercy I've been spared.
   Not by works,
   But by faith in Him who called.
   For so long I've been hindered,
   For so long I've been stalled.

Tangled Up In Blue

Words and Music by Bob Dylan

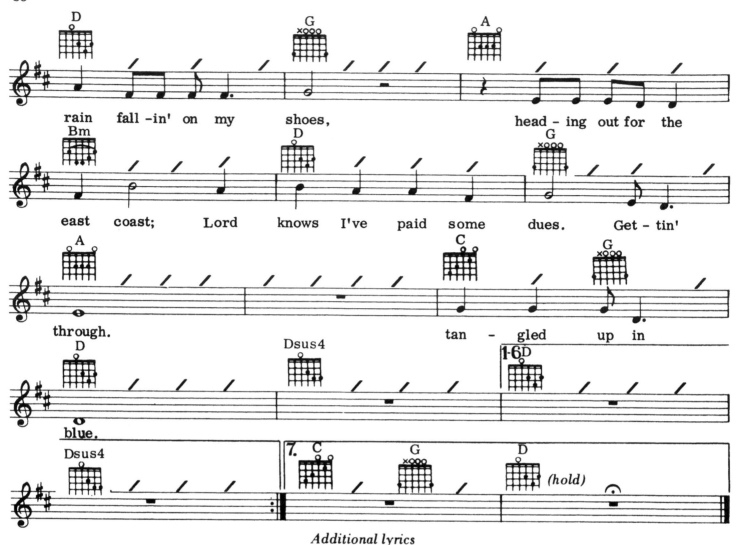

rain fall-in' on my shoes, head-ing out for the east coast; Lord knows I've paid some dues. Get-tin' through. tan - gled up in blue.

Additional lyrics

2. She was married when we first met,
Soon to be divorced.
I helped her out of a jam, I guess,
But I used a little too much force.
We drove that car as far as we could,
Abandoned it out west.
Split up on a dark sad night,
Both agreeing it was best.
She turned around to look at me
As I was walkin' away,
I heard her say over my shoulder,
"We'll meet again some day
On the avenue."
Tangled up in blue.

3. I had a job in the great north woods
Working as a cook for a spell,
But I never did like it all that much
And one day the axe just fell.
So I drifted down to New Orleans
Where I happened to be employed,
Workin' for a while on a fishin' boat
Right outside of Delacroix.
But all the while I was alone
The past was close behind.
I seen a lot of women,
But she never escaped my mind
And I just grew.
Tangled up in blue.

4. She was workin' in a topless place
   And I stopped in for a beer,
   I just kept lookin' at the side of her face
   In the spotlight so clear.
   And later on as the crowd thinned out
   I's just about to do the same,
   She was standing there in back of my chair
   Said to me, "Don't I know your name?"
   I muttered somethin' underneath my breath,
   She studied the lines on my face.
   I must admit I felt a little uneasy
   When she bent down to tie the laces
   Of my shoe.
   Tangled up in blue.

5 She lit a burner on the stove
   And offered me a pipe.
   "I thought you'd never say hello," she said,
   "You look like the silent type."
   Then she opened up a book of poems
   And handed it to me,
   Written by an Italian poet
   From the thirteenth century.
   And every one of them words rang true
   And glowed like burnin' coal,
   Pourin' off of every page
   Like it was written in my soul
   From me to you.
   Tangled up in blue.

6. I lived with them on Montague Street
   In a basement down the stairs;
   There was music in the cafes at night
   And revolution in the air.
   Then he started into dealing with slaves
   And something inside of him died.
   She had to sell everything she owned
   And froze up inside.
   And when finally the bottom fell out
   I became withdrawn,
   The only thing I knew how to do
   Was to keep on keepin' on
   Like a bird that flew.
   Tangled up in blue.

7. So now I'm goin' back again,
   I got to get to her somehow,
   All the people we used to know,
   They're an illusion to me now.
   Some are mathematicians,
   Some are carpenters' wives.
   Don't know how it all got started
   I don't know what they're doin' with their lives.
   But me, I'm still on the road
   Headin' for another joint.
   We always did feel the same,
   We just saw it from a different point
   Of view.
   Tangled up in blue.

Maggie's Farm
Words and Music by Bob Dylan

Moderately, in 2

1. I ain't gon-na work on Mag-gie's farm no more. — No, I ain't gon-na work on Mag-gie's farm no more. — Well, I wake in the morn-ing, fold my hands and pray for rain. I got a head full of i-de-as that are driv-in' me in-sane. — It's a shame, the way she makes me scrub the floor. —

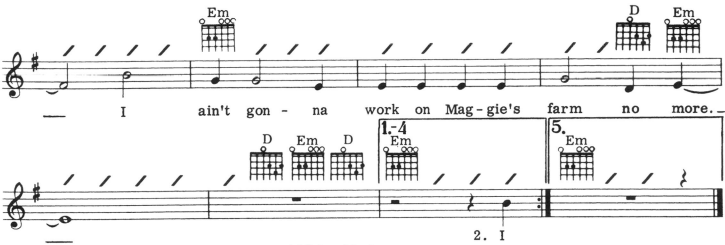

I ain't gon - na work on Mag - gie's farm no more. __

2. I

Additional lyrics

2. I ain't gonna work for Maggie's brother no more.
    No, I ain't gonna work for Maggie's brother no more.
    Well, he hands you a nickel,
    He hands you a dime.
    He asks you with a grin
    If you're havin' a good time,
    Then he fines you every time you slam the door.
    I ain't gonna work for Maggie's brother no more.

3. I ain't gonna work for Maggie's pa no more.
    No, I ain't gonna work for Maggie's pa no more.
    Well, he puts his cigar
    Out in your face just for kicks.
    His bedroom window,
    It is made out of bricks.
    The National Guard stands around his door.
    Ah, I ain't gonna work for Maggie's pa no more.

4. I ain't gonna work for Maggie's ma no more.
    No, I ain't gonna work for Maggie's ma no more.
    Well she talks to all the servants
    About man and God and law.
    Everybody says she's the brains behind pa,
    She's sixty-eight, but she says she's twenty-four.
    I ain't gonna work for Maggie's ma no more.

5. I ain't gonna work on Maggie's farm no more.
    No, I ain't gonna work on Maggie's farm no more.
    Well, I try my best
    To be just like I am,
    But everybody wants you
    To be just like them.
    They sing while you slave
    And I just get bored.
    I ain't gonna work on Maggie's farm no more.

It Ain't Me, Babe

Words and Music by Bob Dylan

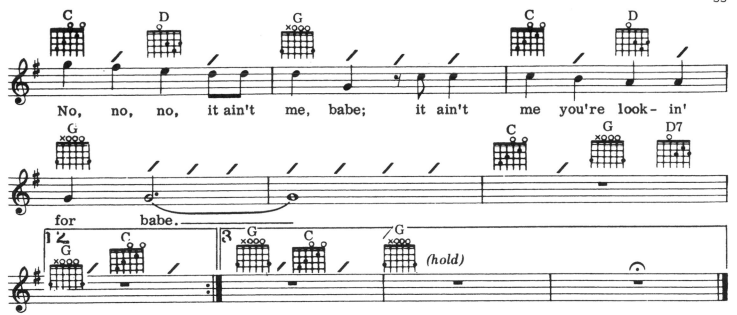

No, no, no, it ain't me, babe; it ain't me you're look-in' for babe. _____

(hold)

Additional lyrics

2. Go lightly from the ledge, babe,
   Go lightly on the ground.
   I'm not the one you want; babe,
   I will only let you down.
   You say you're lookin' for someone
   Who will promise never to part,
   Someone to close his eyes for you
   Someone to close his heart,
   Someone who will die for you an' more:
   But it ain't me, babe.
   No, no, no it ain't me, babe;
   It ain't me your're lookin' for, babe.

3. Go melt back into the night, babe,
   Everything inside is made of stone.
   There's nothing in here moving
   An' anyway I'm not alone.
   You say you're looking for someone
   Who'll pick you up each time you fall,
   To gather flowers constantly
   An' to come each time you call.
   A lover for your life an' nothing more:
   But it ain't me, babe.
   No, no, no it ain't me, babe
   It ain't me you're lookin' for, babe.

I Shall Be Released
Words and Music by Bob Dylan

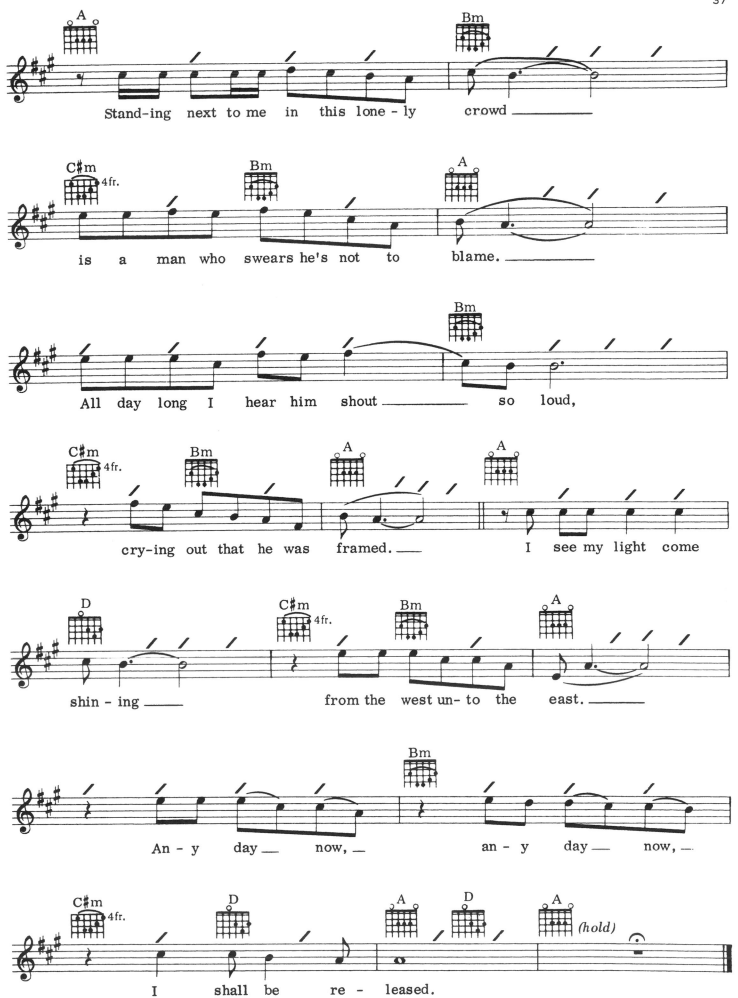

A Hard Rain's A-Gonna Fall

Words and Music by Bob Dylan

Moderately

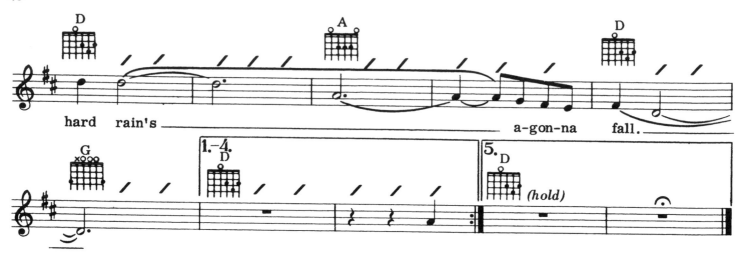

hard rain's _____ a-gon-na fall. _____

Additional lyrics

2. Oh, what did you see, my blue-eyed son?
   Oh, what did you see, my darling young one?

   I saw a new born baby with wild wolves all around it,
   I saw a highway of diamonds with nobody on it,
   I saw a black branch with blood that kept drippin',
   I saw a room full of men with their hammers a-bleedin',
   I saw a white ladder all covered with water,
   I saw ten thousand talkers whose tongues were all broken,
   I saw guns and sharp swords in the hands of young children
   And it's a hard, and it's a hard, it's a hard, it's a hard
   And it's a hard rain's a-gonna fall.

3. And what did you hear, my blue-eyed son?
   And what did you hear, my darling young one?

   I heard the sound of a thunder, it roared out a warnin',
   Heard the roar of a wave that could drown the whole world,
   Heard one hundred drummers whose hands were a-blazin',
   Heard ten thousand whisperin' and nobody listenin',
   Heard one person starve, I heard many people laughin',
   Heard the song of a poet who died in the gutter,
   Heard the sound of a clown who cried in the alley.
   And it's a hard, and it's a hard, it's a hard, it's a hard,
   And it's a hard rain's a-gonna fall.

4.
Oh, who did you meet, my blue-eyed son?
Who did you meet my darling young one?

I met a young child beside a dead pony,
I met a white man who walked a black dog,
I met a young woman whose body was burning,
I met a young girl, she gave me a rainbow,
I met one man who was wounded in love,
I met another man who was wounded with hatred,
And it's a hard, it's a hard, it's a hard, it's a hard,
It's a hard rain's a-gonna fall.

5.
Oh, what'll you do now, my blue-eyed son?
Oh, what'll you do now, my darling young one?

I'm a-goin' back out 'fore the rain starts a-fallin',
I'll walk to the depths of the deepest black forest,
Where the people are many and their hands are all empty,
Where the pellets of poison are flooding their waters,
Where the home in the valley meets the damp dirty prison,
Where the executioner's face is always well hidden,
Where hunger is ugly, where souls are forgotten,
Where black is the color, where none is the number,
And I'll tell it and think it and speak it and breathe it,
And reflect it from the mountain so all souls can see it,
Then I'll stand on the ocean until I start sinkin',
But I'll know my song well before I start singin'.
And it's a hard, it's a hard, it's a hard, it's a hard,
It's a hard rain's a-gonna fall.

Gotta Serve Somebody
Words and Music by Bob Dylan

Moderatley, in 2

1. You may be an am - bas - sa - dor ___ to Eng - land or France. ___ You may like to

gam - ble, you might like to dance.

You may ___ be the heav - y - weight ___ cham -

pion of the world. You may be a

so - cial - ite ___ with a long _____ string of pearls.

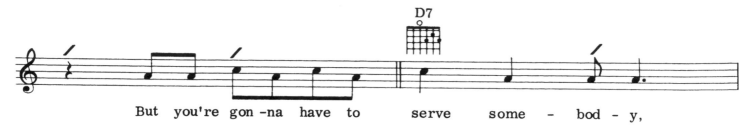

But you're gon -na have to serve some - bod - y,

yes in - deed, you're gon -na have to

serve some - bod -y. Well,

it may be the dev-il, or _____ it may be the

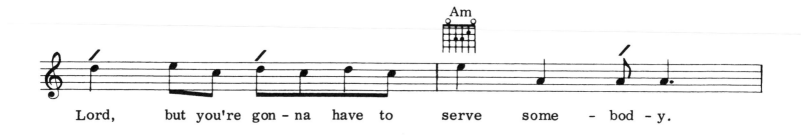

Lord, but you're gon - na have to serve some - bod - y.

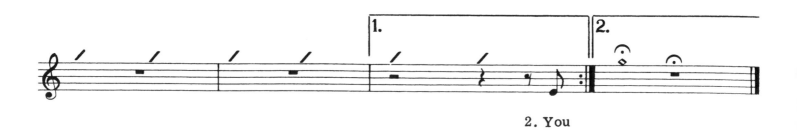

2. You

Additional lyrics

2. You might be a rock 'n' roll addict prancing on the stage.
    You might have drugs at your command, women in a cage.
    You may be a business man or some high degree thief.
    They may call you doctor or they may call you chief.

3. You may be a state trooper, you might be a young Turk.
    You might be the head of some big TV network.
    You may be rich or poor, you may be blind or lame.
    You may be living in another country under another name.

4. You may be a construction worker working on a home.
    You may be living in a mansion or you might live in a dome.
    You might own guns and you might even own tanks.
    You might be somebody's landlord, you might even own banks.

5. You may be a preacher with your spiritual pride.
    You may be a city councilman taking bribes on the side.
    You may be workin' in a barbershop, you may know how to cut hair.
    You may be somebody's mistress, may be somebody's heir.

6. Might like to wear cotton, might like to wear silk.
    Might like to drink whiskey, might like to drink milk.
    You might like to eat caviar, you might like to eat bread.
    You may be sleeping on the floor, sleeping in a king-sized bed.

7. You may call me Terry, you may call me Timmy.
    You may call me Bobby, you may call me Zimmy;
    You may call me R.J., you may call me Ray.
    You may call me anything but no matter what you say,

POSITIVELY 4TH STREET

Words and Music by Bob Dylan

win - ning. _____

Additional lyrics

2. You say I let you down,
   You know it's not like that.
   If you're so hurt
   Why then don't you show it.
   You say you lost your faith,
   But that's not where it's at.
   You had no faith to lose
   And you know it.

3. I know the reason
   That you talk behind my back,
   I used to be among the crowd
   You're in with,
   Do you take me for such a fool
   To think I'd make contact
   With the one who tries to hide
   When he don't know to begin with.

4. You see me on the street,
   You always act surprised.
   You say, "How are you?","Good luck".
   But you don't mean it.
   When you know as well as me
   You'd rather see me paralyzed,
   Why don't you just come out once
   And scream it.

5. No, I do not feel that good
   When I see the heart breaks you embrace.
   If I was a master thief
   Perhaps I'd rob them.
   And now I know you're dissatisfied
   With your position and your place.
   Don't you understand,
   It's not my problem.

6. I wish that for just one time
   You could stand inside my shoes,
   And just for that one moment
   I could be you.
   Yes, I wish that for just one time
   You could stand inside my shoes;
   You'd know what a drag it is
   To see you.

LAY, LADY, LAY

WORDS AND MUSIC BY BOB DYLAN

Moderately, in 2

1. Lay, la-dy, lay, ___ lay a-cross my big brass bed. ____

Lay, la-dy, lay, ___ lay a-cross my big brass bed. ____

What-ev - er col - ors you have in your mind, I'll show them to

you and you'll see them shine.

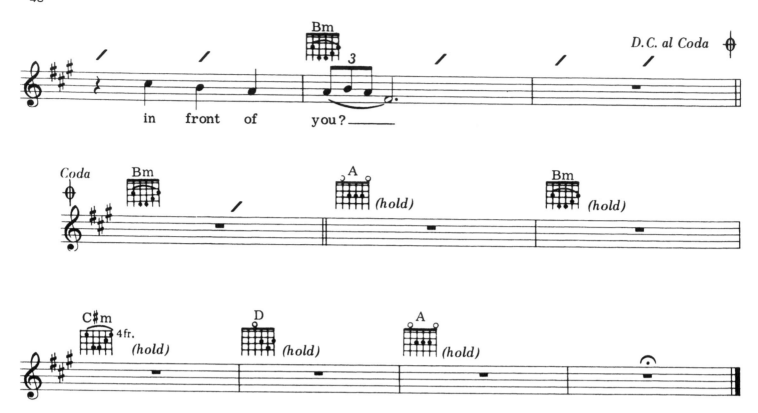

in front of you?

Coda

Additional lyrics

2. Stay, lady, stay,
   Stay with your man awhile.
   Until the break of day,
   Let me see you make him smile.
   His clothes are dirty, but his hands are clean
   And you're the best thing that he's ever seen.
   Stay, lady, stay,
   Stay with your man awhile.

3. Lay, lady, lay,
   Lay across my big brass bed.
   Stay, lady, stay,
   Stay while the night is still ahead.
   I long to see you in the morning light,
   I long to reach for you in the night.
   Stay, lady, stay,
   Stay while the night is still ahead.

Hurricane
Words and Music by Bob Dylan

Moderately

(Guitar)

1. Pis - tol shots ring out in the

bar - room night. _ En - ter Pat - ty Val - en-tine from the

up - per hall. _ She sees the bar-tend - er in a

pool of blood, _ cries out "My God, they

killed them all!" Here comes the sto - ry of the

Hur - ri - cane, _ the man the au - thor- i -ties

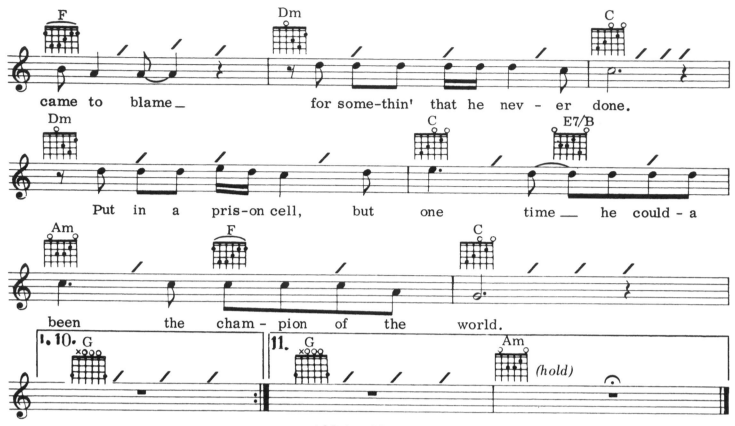

came to blame — for some-thin' that he nev - er done.
Put in a pris-on cell, but one time — he could - a
been the cham - pion of the world.

Additional lyrics

2. Three bodies lyin' there does Patty see
   And another man named Bello, movin' around mysteriously.
   "I didn't do it, "he says, and he throws up his hands
   "I saw only robbin' the register, I hope you understand.
   I saw them leavin, "he says, and he stops.
   "One of us had better call up the cops."
   And so Patty calls the cops
   And they arrive on the scene with their red lights flashin'
   In the hot New Jersey night.

3. Meanwhile, far away in another part of town
   Rubin Carter and a couple of friends are drivin' around.
   Number one contender for the middleweight crown
   Had no idea what kinda shit was about to go down,
   When a cop pulled him over to the side of the road.
   Just like the time before and the time before that,
   In Paterson that's just the way things go.
   If you're black you might as well not show up on the street
   'Less you wanta draw the heat.

4. Alfred Bello had a partner and he had a rap for the cops:
   Him and Arthur Dexter Bradley were just out prowlin' around.
   He said, "I saw two men runnin' out, they looked like middleweights.
   They jumped into a white car with out-of-state plates,"
   And Miss Patty Valentine just nodded her head.
   Cop said, "Wait a minute boys, this one's not dead."
   So they took him to the infirmary
   And though this man could hardly see
   They told him that he could identify the guilty men.

5. Four in the mornin' and they haul Rubin in,
   Take him to the hospital and they bring him upstairs.
   The wounded man looks up through his one dyin' eye
   Says, "Wha'd you bring him in here for? He ain't the guy!"
   Yes, here's the story of the Hurricane,
   The man the authorities came to blame
   For somethin' that he never done.
   Put in a prison cell, but one time he coulda been
   The champion of the world.

6. Four months later, the ghettoes are in flame.
   Rubin's in South America, fightin' for his name.
   While Arthur Dexter Bradley's still in the robbery game
   And the cops are puttin' the screws to him, lookin' for somebody to blame.
   "Remember that murder that happened in a bar?"
   "Remember you said you saw the getaway car?"
   "You think you'd like to play ball with the law?"
   "Think it mighta been that fighter that you saw runnin' that night?"
   "Don't forget that you are white."

7. Arthur Dexter Bradley said, "I'm really not sure."
   Cops said, "A poor boy like you could use a break.
   We got you for the motel job and we're talkin' to your friend Bello.
   Now you don't wanta have to go back to jail, be a nice fellow.
   You'll be doin' society a favor,
   That sonofabitch is brave and gettin' braver.
   We want to put his ass in stir,
   We want to pin this triple murder on him,
   He ain't no Gentleman Jim."

8. Rubin could take a man out with just one punch,
   But he never did like to talk about it all that much.
   It's my work, he'd say, and I do it for pay.
   And when it's over I'd just as soon go on my way
   Up to some paradise,
   Where the trout streams flow and the air is nice
   And ride a horse along a trail.
   But then they took him to the jail house,
   Where they try to turn a man into a mouse.

9. All of Rubin's cards were marked in advance.
   The trial was a pig-circus, he never had a chance.
   The judge made Rubin's witnesses drunkards from the slums,
   To the white folks who watched he was a revolutionary bum.
   And to the black folks he was just a crazy nigger,
   No one doubted that he pulled the trigger,
   And though they could not produce the gun
   The D.A. said he was the one who did the deed
   And the all-white jury agreed.

10.
Rubin Carter was falsely tried.
The crime was murder "one", guess who testified?
Bello and Bradley and they both baldly lied
And the newspapers, they all went along for the ride.
How can the life of such a man
Be in the palm of some fool's hand?
To see him obviously framed
Couldn't help but make me feel ashamed to live in a land
Where justice is a game.

11.
Now all the criminals in their coats and their ties
Are free to drink martinis and watch the sun rise
While Rubin sits like Buddha in a ten-foot cell,
An innocent man in a living hell.
That's the story of the Hurricane,
But it won't be over till they clear his name
And give him back the time he's done.
Put in a prison cell, but one time he coulda been
The champion of the world.

Highway 61 Revisited

Words and Music by Bob Dylan

Six - ty - one."

Additional lyrics

2. Well Georgia Sam, he had a bloody nose.
Welfare Department they wouldn't give him no clothes.
He asked poor Howard, where can I go?
Howard said there's only one place I know.
Sam said tell me quick man I got to run.
Ol' Howard just pointed with his gun
And said that way down on Highway 61.

3. Well Mack the Finger said to Louie the King,
I got forty red white and blue shoe strings
And a thousand telephones that don't ring.
Do you know where I can get rid of these things?
And Louie the King said let me think for a minute son,
And he said yes, I think it can be easily done.
Just take everything down to Highway 61.

4. Now the fifth daughter on the twelfth night
Told the first father that things weren't right.
My complexion, she said, is much too white.
He said, come here and step into the light, he says, hmm you're right.
Let me tell the second mother this has been done.
But the second mother was with the seventh son
And they were both out on Highway 61.

5. Now the rovin' gambler, he was very bored.
He was tryin' to create a next world war.
He found a promoter who nearly fell off the floor.
He said, I never engaged in this kind of thing before,
But yes, I think it can be very easily done.
We'll just put some bleachers out in the sun
And have it on Highway 61.

Shelter From The Storm
Words and Music by Bob Dylan

Moderately fast

1. 'Twas in an-oth-er life-time, one of toil and blood, when black-ness was a vir-tue and the road was full of mud. _____ I came in from _ the wil-der-ness, a crea-ture void _ of form, _____ "Come in," she said, "I'll give you shel-ter from _ the storm." 2. And if I pass _ this way a-gain you can rest _ a-sured _____

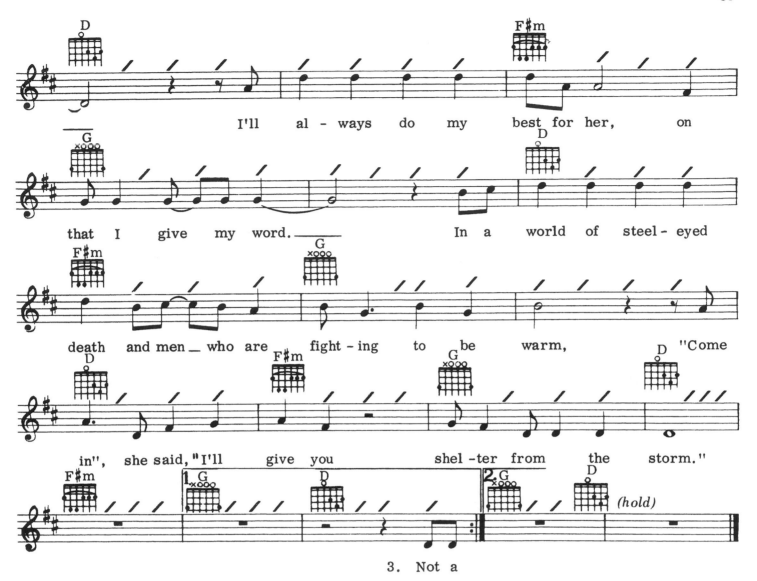

I'll al-ways do my best for her, on that I give my word. In a world of steel-eyed death and men who are fight-ing to be warm, "Come in", she said, "I'll give you shel-ter from the storm."

3. Not a

Additional lyrics

3. Not a word was spoken between us,
   There was little risk involved;
   Everything up to that point
   Had been left unresolved.
   Try imagining a place
   Where it's always safe and warm,
   "Come in", she said, "I'll give you
   Shelter from the storm."

4. I was burned out from exhaustion,
   Buried in the hail,
   Poisoned in the bushes
   An' blown out on the trail.
   Hunted like a crocodile,
   Ravaged in the corn,
   "Come in", she said, "I'll give you
   Shelter from the storm."

5. Suddenly I turned around
   And she was standin' there
   With silver bracelts on her wrists
   And flowers in her hair.
   She walked up to me so gracefully
   And took my crown of thorns,
   "Come in," she said, "I'll give you
   Shelter from the storm."

6. Now there's a wall between us,
   Somethin' there's been lost;
   I took too much for granted,
   Got my signals crossed.
   Just to think that it all began
   On a long forgotten morn,
   "Come in," she said, "I'll give you
   Shelter from the storm."

7. Well, the deputy walks on hard nails
   And the preacher rides a mount;
   But nothing really matters much,
   It's doom alone that counts.
   And the one-eyed undertaker,
   He blows a futile horn,
   "Come in," she said, "I'll give you
   Shelter from the storm".

8. I've heard new-born babies wailin'
   Like a mornin' dove,
   And old men with broken teeth
   Stranded without love.
   Do I understand your question, man,
   Is it hopeless and forlorn?
   "Come in," she said, "I'll give you
   Shelter from the storm."

9. In a little hill top village
   They gambled for my clothes;
   I bargained for salvation
   An' they gave me a lethal dose.
   I offered up my innocence
   And got repaid with scorn,
   "Come in," she said, "I'll give you
   Shelter from the storm."

10. Well, I'm livin' in a foreign country,
    But I'm bound to cross the line;
    Beauty walks a razor's edge,
    Someday I'll make it mine.
    If I could only turn back the clock
    To when God and her were born,
    "Come in," she said, "I'll give you
    Shelter from the storm."